Julie,

You are the best sister anyone could ask for, and I love you very much. Remember you are a wonderful mother, sister, and friend. If that little baby you are carrying is a girl, I hope Emily and she will have a relationship as loving as ours, if it is a boy, you'll just have to have another girl so Emily will be blessed as I am to have a "little sister"

Always remember how proud I am of you, God has blessed me, by giving me you! Love, Cindy

Dedicated to Alicia

Published by C.R. Gibson® Norwalk, CT 06856
C.R. Gibson® is a registered trademark of Thomas Nelson, Inc.
Made in the U.S.A.
ISBN 0-7667-0953-1
GB649

To My Sister

photographs by

Kim Anderson

poetry by Julie Mitchell Marra

THE C.R. GIBSON COMPANY, NORWALK, CONNECTICUT

$\mathcal{W}$ithout you,
growing up
would not have been the same.

Over the years
we have shared so much
and built a relationship
that is precious and lasting.

We have shared
ice cream at the beach,
popcorn at the movies,
and hot dogs on the sidewalk.

We have shared
amusement park rides,
splashing in puddles
in the rain,
sledding, skating —

and making angels in the snow.

With you
I can laugh
I can cry
I can say what's on my mind
or just be silent.

With you
it's easy to be me.

I remember disagreements...

saying things we didn't really mean.

I also remember that
only hours later
we were laughing
so hard
we cried.

Sometimes when life seems difficult...

I remember our childhood days
full of laughter and love.
Then I am able to lift my spirits
and lighten my outlook.

The memories we share
remind me
of how lucky I am
to have a sister
like you.

People we meet see
a little of you in me
and a little of me in you.

I look at you
and my eyes look back.
I speak
and I hear your voice.

We are more than merely acquaintances...

it's as if we are cut
from the same fabric.

We have a common thread
that won't be broken—
by people
or years
or distance.

We are never at a loss for words.

We can talk for hours about
nothing at all or communicate
the deepest hurt
with a single word.
With you, speech is effortless
and laughter is contagious.

You bring
love and light,
kindness and caring,
cheer and support
into my life.

We do not always see
eye to eye...

Sometimes we take different roads.

Our relationship is not always perfect,
but when we have a problem
it's surmountable.

Sometimes we are the mirror image
of each other
and other times
we couldn't be more opposite.

But because of you,
I know myself better.

I know that if I pick up the phone,
you'll be there.

If I need help,
you'll give it to me twofold.

If I start to go down the wrong path,
you'll try to lead me the right way.

There's no end to what you do for me
and I want you to know
I'll do the same for you.

$\mathcal{T}$hank you for listening
without judging,
and for giving advice
without pushing.

Thank you for helping me
gain confidence in myself
to stand alone—
and for letting me know you'll
always be there.

The greatest part about being sisters
is sharing ourselves.

Having our own interests,
but always communicating.

Striving to meet our own goals,
but never losing sight of one another

Living our own lives,
but always remaining connected.

*You and I have so
many memories...*

you share my history.

You remember where I've been,
respect who I've become
and encourage me where I'm going.

I know that our relationship will grow stronger year after year.

and I hope that all of the blessings you bring to my life—
I can return to you.

*M*ay you always be fulfilled.

May you feel content with
your accomplishments
and, no matter what,
know that you are truly and
deeply loved.

You are my sister and my best friend!

COLOPHON:
Edited by Eileen Mulkerin D'Andrea
Designed by Millicent Iacono
Type set in ITC Garamond Light and Charme